Best Kids' Christmas Jokes EVER!

Highlights Press
Honesdale, Pennsylvania

Cover Art by Neil Numberman
Contributing Illustrators: David Coulson, Mike Dammer, Kelly Kennedy,
Pat Lewis, Mike Moran, Neil Numberman, Rich Powell, Kevin Rechin,
Rick Stromoski, Pete Whitehead

For information about permission to reprint selections from this book,
please contact permissions@highlights.com.

Published by Highlights Press
815 Church Street
Honesdale, Pennsylvania 18431
ISBN: 978-1-64472-120-9

Library of Congress Control Number: 2020935561
Printed in Mattoon, IL, USA
Mfg. 05/2020

First edition
Visit our website at Highlights.com.
10 9 8 7 6 5 4 3 2 1

CONTENTS

SILLY SNOW

What did one snowman say to the other?

"Do you smell carrots?"

Where do snowpeople dance?

At a snowball

Knock, knock.

Who's there?

Snow.

Snow who?

Snow one's better than you.

What do you call a snowman in Florida?

Water

Ann: Hooray! The teacher said we will have a test, rain or shine.

Dan: Then why are you so happy?

Ann: It's snowing!

Where do hockey players go to get a new uniform?

New Jersey

Knock, knock.

Who's there?

Rufus.

Rufus who?

Rufus covered in snow. Let me in before it slides off!

Where did the snowman want to go on vacation?

Somewhere cold

What do snowpeople call their offspring?

Chill-dren

What is Frosty the Snowman's favorite side dish?

Cold-slaw

What is the hardest foot to buy a skate for?

A square foot

What did the snowman do when he got upset?

He had a meltdown.

Noelle: Ouch! My new boots hurt when I walk in them.

Brooke: No wonder! You have them on the wrong feet.

Noelle: But I don't have any other feet!

Why is lava red hot?

Because if it were cold and white, it would be snow

Which figure skater can jump higher than the judge's table?

All of them—a table can't jump.

What's white and goes up?

A confused snowflake

Knock, knock.

Who's there?

Snow.

Snow who?

**Snow skating today—
the ice is too thin.**

What do snowmen wear on
their heads?

Ice caps

Emmy: May I share your sled?

Mike: Sure. We'll go half and half.

Emmy: Thanks.

Mike: I'll have it for downhill, and you can have
it for uphill.

In what sport do you sit
down going up and stand
up going down?

Skiing

Why was Cinderella such a bad figure skater?

Her coach was a pumpkin.

What is a snowman's favorite cereal?

Frosted Snowflakes

Which figure skater has the biggest skates?

The one with the biggest feet

What do you call Frosty the Snowman in May?

A puddle

Knock, knock.

Who's there?

Snowy.

Snowy who?

Snowy in the word *snow*—it's spelled s-n-o-w.

Why shouldn't you wear snow boots?

Because they melt

Why does a skating rink get warm after a competition?

Because all the fans have left

What happened when the snowwoman got angry at the snowman?

She gave him the cold shoulder.

What is a snowman's favorite food?

A brrr-ito

Why did the skier take up ice-skating?

She was snow bored.

How do snowpeople greet each other?

"Ice to meet you!"

Knock, knock.

Who's there?

Alaska.

Alaska who?

Alaska my parents if I can go sledding!

What did one snowman say to the other snowman?

"You're cool."

Why did the boy only wear one snow boot?

There was only a 50 percent chance of snow.

Why did the snowplow driver enjoy her work?

Because there's no business like snow business

What did one snowman say to the other?

I couldn't hear them, so I have snow idea!

Who is Frosty the Snowman's favorite aunt?

Aunt Arctica

What did the skeleton drive to the ice rink?

A zam-bony

When is a boat just like snow?

When it's adrift

What is a snowman's favorite game?

Freeze-bee

Why did the boy keep his trumpet out in the snow?

Because he liked cool music

What do penguins do when they meet someone new?

They say something to break the ice.

What would you get if you crossed a snowball with a vampire?

Frostbite

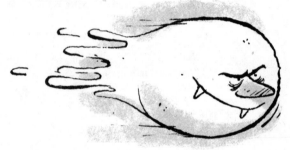

MERRY MUSIC

Knock, knock.

Who's there?

Guitar.

Guitar who?

Let's guitar coats—it's cold out there!

What is a librarian's favorite Christmas carol?

"Silent Night"

Why is everyone so thirsty at the North Pole?

No-well, no-well!

Knock, knock.

Who's there?

Hannah.

Hannah who?

"Hannah partridge in a pear tree . . ."

What has 40 feet and sings?

20 Christmas carolers

What song do you sing at a snowman's Christmas party?

"Freeze a Jolly Good Fellow"

What's a short dog's favorite Christmas song lyric?

"Dachshund through the snow . . ."

Knock, knock.

Who's there?

Megan and chicken.

Megan and chicken who?

"He's Megan a list and chicken it twice, he's gonna find out who's naughty or nice . . ."

How can you tell carolers are coming to your house?

They jingle all the way.

What do you call an insect who loves Christmas carols?

A humbug

What is a skunk's favorite Christmas song?

"Jingle Smells"

Knock, knock.

Who's there?

Noel.

Noel who?

Noel-bows on the table, please.

What do fish sing at Christmas time?

Christmas corals

How does Good King Wenceslas like his pizza?

Deep pan crisp and even

What's a boat's favorite Christmas carol?

"Dock the Halls"

What do you give carolers when they sing for you?

Some har-money

How does butter's favorite Christmas song go?

"You butter not shout, you butter not cry!"

Knock, knock.

Who's there?

Mime.

Mime who?

"Mime dreaming of a white Christmas."

What is a sheep's favorite Christmas song?

"All I Want for Christmas Is Ewe"

Why couldn't the caroler get into his apartment?

He could never find the right keys.

Knock, knock.

Who's there?

Dexter.

Dexter who?

"Dexter halls with boughs of holly . . ."

What did the farmer see when he found his stallion in the bathtub?

One-horse, soap-and hay

What carol is heard in the desert?

"Camel Ye Faithful"

Knock, knock.

Who's there?

Honda.

Honda who?

"Honda first day of Christmas, my true love gave to me . . ."

What happens when the Christmas musicians lose their beat?

They have a tempo-tantrum.

What is a lightning bolt's favorite Christmas song?

"Shocking Around the Christmas Tree"

Who gets invited to the most holiday parties?

Christmas Carol

Which state has the most singers on Christmas Eve?

North Carol-ina

Knock, knock.

Who's there?

Ivana.

Ivana who?

"Ivana wish you a merry Christmas!"

What is a Christmas tree's favorite Christmas carol?

"We Needle-ittle Christmas"

What do you get when you put chocolate on a harp?

Sweet music

What is a duck's favorite ballet?

The Nut-quacker

Knock, knock.

Who's there?

Irish.

Irish who?

"Irish you a Merry Christmas . . ."

Susie: Do you know the names of any angels?

Jacob: Just Herald— "Hark! The Herald angel sings . . ."

How do sheep who speak Spanish say "Merry Christmas"?

"Fleece Navidad"

ENTERTAINING ELVES

What is an elf's favorite kind of music?

Gift rap

What kind of photos do elves take?

Elfies

What do you call an elf who steals gift wrap from the rich and gives it to the poor?

Ribbon Hood

Where do you find elves?

Depends where you left them!

What is an elf's favorite sport?

North-pole vaulting

How many of Santa's helpers does it take to make a dozen?

Tw-elf

Why did the elf cross the road?

Because he was riding a chicken

What kind of money do elves use?

Jingle bills

What do you call an elf who's won the lottery?

Welfy

Who is an elf's favorite character in *A Christmas Carol*?

Tiny Tim

How do elves get from floor to floor?

In the elf-avator

What do elves do after school?

Gnome-work

If athletes get athlete's foot, what do elves get?

Mistle-toes

What is an elf's favorite sport?

Mini golf

Knock, knock.

Who's there?

Elf shoe.

Elf shoe who?

Elf the shoe fits, then wear it!

Why do elves know so many secrets?

Because they're all ears

What kind of bread do elves make sandwiches with?

Why, shortbread of course!

Santa rides in a sleigh. What do elves ride in?

Minivans

What is a dozen Santa's helpers minus one?

Elf-even

What do elves learn in school?

The elf-abet

How do elves greet each other?

"Small world, isn't it?"

What type of cars do elves drive?

Toy-otas

What is an elf's favorite type of painting?

An elf-portrait

Why did the elf win the argument about his ears?

He had some good points.

What do the elves call it when Saint Nick claps his hands at the end of a play?

Santapplause

What was the elf allergic to?

Sh-elf-ish

Why did the elf put her bed into the fireplace?

She wanted to sleep like a log.

What do you call an elf wearing earmuffs?

*Anything you want.
He can't hear you!*

What do you call a greedy elf?

Elfish

Who lives at the North Pole, makes toys, and rides around in a pumpkin?

Cinder-elf-a

Why did Santa reward his helpers?

To give them more elf-esteem

What do the elves eat with?

U-tinsel-s

Who is an elf's favorite singer?

Elf-is Presley

What do you call a Santa's helper who always interrupts people?

Rude-elf

How long are an elf's legs?

Long enough to reach the ground

How many elves does it take to change a light bulb?

Eight. One to change the bulb and seven to stand on each other's shoulders!

HILARIOUS HOLLY

Why did the dinosaur eat the Christmas lights?

Because he wanted a light snack

What does a fish hang on its door at Christmas?

A coral wreath

What happens if you eat Christmas decorations?

You get tinsel-itus.

Knock, knock.

Who's there?

Snow.

Snow who?

Snow use—I'll never finish decorating on time.

What did the audience see after Holly's performance?

The bows of Holly

How does a polar bear decorate for Christmas?

With mistle-snow

Where is a cat when the Christmas lights go out?

In the dark

What did Thomas Jefferson put up for Christmas?

The Decoration of Independence

What has green leaves, red berries, and smells fishy?

Holly mackerel!

Liam: Why are you switching out the good light bulbs?

Mom: You might not think it makes a big difference, but it could make a whole watt!

Where did the mistletoe go to become famous?

Holly-wood

What do mallards hang up for the holidays?

Duck-orations

What kind of jokes does a popcorn garland love?

Corny ones

What did the ornament say to the star on top of the tree?

"You light up my life."

Knock, knock.

Who's there?

Diesel.

Diesel who?

Diesel be the best decorations ever!

What do reindeer hang on their Christmas trees?

Horn-aments

What did the happy light bulb say to the sad light bulb?

"Why don't you lighten up?"

How did the Advent candle lose its job?

It got fired.

What's green, covered in tinsel, and goes *croak*?

A mistle-toad

What happened to the dog when he swallowed a strand of Christmas lights?

He barked with de-light.

Knock, knock.

Who's there?

Aretha.

Aretha who?

Aretha holly would look nice on your front door.

How do you decorate a canoe for Christmas?

With oar-naments

What should you do if your car breaks down on Christmas Eve?

Get a mistle-tow.

Christmas Light #1: You've gotten taller since I last saw you.

Christmas Light #2: I guess I'm having a glow spurt!

TICKLISH TREATS

Santa: What is this fly doing on my ice cream?

Waiter: I believe it's downhill skiing, sir.

Knock, knock.

Who's there?

Howdy.

Howdy who?

Howdy-licious is Christmas dinner?

Why did the Christmas cookie go to the doctor?

She felt crumby.

What do you use to drain your Christmas brussels sprouts?

An Advent colander

What beverage is always tardy on Christmas?

Hot choco-late

Why is fruitcake like a history book?

Because it's full of dates

Mom: Did you eat all the Christmas cookies?

Hope: No, I didn't touch one.

Mom: Then why is there only one left?

Hope: That's the one I didn't touch.

What's red, white, and blue?

A sad candy cane

Why was the gingerbread cookie robbed?

Because of its dough

Knock, knock.

Who's there?

Pecan.

Pecan who?

Pecan somebody your own size.

What do baseball and Christmas cookies have in common?

They both need the batter.

What's the best thing to put into Christmas dinner?

Your teeth!

Samantha: Why was the Christmas cookie sad?

Sophia: Because that's the way the cookie crumbles?

Samantha: No, because his mother was a wafer so long.

What type of gingerbread people can fly?

The plane ones

How do snowpeople decorate their Christmas cookies?

With icing

Knock, knock.

Who's there?

Grover.

Grover who?

Grover there and get me a candy cane, please.

What does a cookie say when it's excited?

"Chip, chip, hooray!"

Where do gingerbread people sleep?

Under cookie sheets

Why do basketball players love gingerbread cookies?

Because they can dunk them

What did the fruitcake do during Christmas break?

It loafed around.

What's a turkey's favorite Christmas dessert?

Cherry gobbler

Knock, knock.

Who's there?

Stirrup.

Stirrup who?

Stirrup some hot chocolate for me, please.

Charlie: What's your dog's name?

Chelsea: Ginger.

Charlie: Does Ginger bite?

Chelsea: No, but Ginger snaps.

What do sea serpents like in their Christmas cookies?

Chocolate ships

What do gingerbread people use to trim their fingernails?

Cookie cutters

Knock, knock.

Who's there?

Effie.

Effie who?

Effie'd known you were coming, he'd have baked more Christmas treats.

Why did the girl put Christmas cookies under her pillow?

She wanted to have sweet dreams.

What's a mathematician's favorite Christmas snack?

Mince pi

Aliyah: I have a super-secret recipe for Christmas cookies.

Beckett: What is it?

Aliyah: I can't tell you. It's on a knead to dough basis.

What did the happy chocolate say to the cranky chocolate?

"Don't have a meltdown yet! The fondue will be served in an hour."

Knock, knock.

Who's there?

Phillip.

Phillip who?

Phillip my dinner plate, please. I'm starving!

Why does Santa eat so many cookies?

Be-Claus he likes them!

Josh: How was your Christmas, Archie?

Archie: Great! We had Grandma for dinner!

Who was the most dangerous cookie?

The ninja-bread man

What do you call someone who's crazy about hot chocolate?

A cocoa-nut

Knock, knock.

Who's there?

Frostbite.

Frostbite who?

Frostbite your food, then chew it.

What do you call a house full of cakes and cookies?

Dessert-ed

Ella: Did you hear the story about the Christmas cookie?

Bella: No.

Ella: That's OK. It was a crumby story anyway.

Why do baseball players make bad Christmas dinner guests?

They're always stepping on your plates.

What's a math teacher's favorite kind of Christmas candy?

Measure-mints

Knock, knock.

Who's there?

Duncan.

Duncan who?

Duncan cookies in milk tastes good.

What do you call someone who steals snickerdoodles?

A crook-ie

What is the last thing a snowman does when he bakes a cake?

He frosts it.

Riley: This fruitcake tastes funny!

Miley: Then why aren't you laughing?

Who hides in the bakery at Christmas?

A mince spy

What did the cinnamon bread dough say to the baker?

"I don't need you. You knead me!"

What's Santa's favorite candy?

Jolly Ranchers

Why didn't the gingerbread man need glasses?

He had two good raisins.

Knock, knock.

Who's there?

Handsome.

Handsome who?

Handsome of those Christmas cookies over, please. I'm hungry!

What do doctors give gingerbread people when they sprain their ankles?

Candy canes

What gets served on Christmas but never eaten?

The guests

Mom: Do you want the right half of this cookie?

Ezra: Sure—I certainly don't want the wrong half!

What do you sing when the Christmas cookies are in the oven?

"Jingle smells, jingle smells . . ."

Why shouldn't you buy broken candy canes?

Because they aren't in mint condition

Knock, knock.

Who's there?

Atomic.

Atomic who?

I have atomic ache from all the Christmas sweets.

WACKY WINTER

What do polar bears do on the computer?

They surf the winternet.

How far is it from September to December?

Just a short fall

Knock, knock.

Who's there?

Dakota.

Dakota who?

Dakota is too short in the arms for me.

Why do birds fly south for the winter?

Because it's too far to walk

What did the scarf say to the hat?

"You go on ahead."

Knock, knock.

Who's there?

Emma.

Emma who?

Emma bit cold out here.

What athlete is warmest in winter?

A long jumper

How do snowpeople travel around?

By icicle

What is another name for a backwards somersault?

A wintersault

Customer: I'd like to buy a winter coat.

Store clerk: How long?

Customer: For the whole winter.

What kind of vegetables do you pick in the winter?

Snow peas

What did the snowflake say to the fallen leaf?

"You're so last season."

What triangles are the coldest in winter?

Ice-osceles triangles

When are your eyes not eyes?

When the winter wind makes them water

Knock, knock.

Who's there?

Hansel.

Hansel who?

Hansel freeze out here if you don't wear gloves.

What do dinosaurs wear when it's cold outside?

Jurassic Parkas

Why should you never tell a joke while ice-skating?

Because the ice will crack up

First dog: Where do fleas go in the winter?

Second dog: Search me!

Why did Capri go outside with her purse open?

She was expecting some change in the weather.

What do you have in December that you don't have in any other month?

The letter D

How do you tell the weather on Christmas morning?

Look out the window.

What is the coldest month of the year?

Decem-brrrr

Eileen: Is your house warm this winter?

Terry: Yes. The painter gave it two coats.

Knock, knock.

Who's there?

Lemmy.

Lemmy who?

Lemmy put on my coat before we go outside.

Which moves faster in winter: heat or cold?

Heat! It's easy to catch cold.

What did the Jedi say to the grass when it started getting cold outside?

"May the frost be with you."

What do you call a skier who doesn't go fast?

A slope-poke

Knock, knock.

Who's there?

Arthur.

Arthur who?

Arthur-mometer is broken!

What happens when you drop a snowball in water?

It gets wet.

Why did Scrooge freeze his money outside in the winter?

He wanted cold, hard cash.

What's a turtle's favorite thing to wear in winter?

A turtleneck

Why do bears sleep all winter?

Because no one's brave enough to wake them up

Why was the polar bear upset with her test grades?

They were all twenty below zero.

ANIMAL ANTICS

If two fish try out for the Christmas concert, which one will be chosen?

The one with better scales

What do you call a cat that goes to the beach on Christmas?

Sandy Claws

What is a tiger's favorite Christmas carol?

"Jungle Bells"

What color socks do polar bears wear?

They don't wear socks. They have bear feet!

Ashley: What did one cow say to the other cow on Christmas Day?

Melissa: Dairy Christmas!

What is an ape's favorite cookie?

Chocolate chimp

How does a polar bear build its house?

Igloos it together.

What do angry mice send to each other at Christmas?

Cross-mouse cards

What's black and white and blue all over?

A shivering penguin

Knock, knock.

Who's there?

Duck.

Duck who?

"Duck the halls with boughs of holly!"

Why did Scrooge keep a pet lamb?

Because it said, "Baaaaahhh humbug!"

What's a penguin's favorite movie?

Frozen

How do you greet a chihuahua at Christmas?

Feliz Navi-dog!

What is 20 feet tall, has sharp teeth, and goes "Ho, ho, ho?"

Tyranno-santa rex

Where do you find polar bears?

It depends on where you lost them.

What does the cow play on Christmas?

Christmas moo-sic

Did you hear about the cat that swallowed Mrs. Claus's yarn?

She had mittens!

Why did the dog leap for joy?

Joy was holding the Christmas cookies.

What did the snake give to his child on Christmas Eve?

A goodnight hiss

How does a dog stop a Christmas movie?

He presses the paws button.

Why do polar bears have fur coats?

Because they would look silly in ski jackets

Knock, knock.

Who's there?

Chicken.

Chicken who?

**Better chicken the oven—
Christmas dinner's burning!**

Mel: What kind of bank does a penguin go to?

Minnie: I don't know. What kind?

Mel: A snowbank.

**What do sheep say to
each other at Christmas?**

"Merry Christmas to ewe!"

Why don't penguins fly?

They don't have pilots licenses.

What Christmas song do dogs like?

"Bark! The Herald Angels Sing"

How do you keep a polar bear from charging?

Take away its power cord.

Why is a giraffe a bad guest for Christmas dinner?

It eats, leaves.

What do alpacas sing at Christmas time?

"Fa-la-la-la-la, la-la-llama"

What's a bird's favorite Christmas story?

How the Finch Stole Christmas

Knock, knock.

Who's there?

Aurora.

Aurora who?

Aurora's just come from that big polar bear!

Why did the turkey turn down Christmas dessert?

He was already stuffed.

Why do penguins carry fish in their beaks?

Because they don't have any pockets

What's the difference between a polar bear and a banana?

You'd better find out before you try to peel a polar bear.

What's big, white, furry, and always points north?

A polar bearing

Knock, knock.

Who's there?

Iguana.

Iguana who?

"Iguana wish you a Merry Christmas!"

What does a dog breeder get when crossing an Irish Setter with an English Pointer?

A Pointsetter

What's big and white and lives in the Sahara Desert?

A lost polar bear

TREE
TEE-HEES

**What do you get when you cross
a Christmas tree and a dog?**

A fur tree

How do Christmas trees like ice cream served?

In a pinecone

What did the oak tree say to the Christmas tree?

"Stop needling me, or I'm going to leaf you!"

What did the Jedi say to the Christmas tree?

"May the forest be with you."

Why are Christmas trees such bad knitters?

They are always dropping their needles.

What did the Christmas tree do when the bank closed?

It started its own branch.

Liam: How did you get that scratch?

Sampson: See that branch on the Christmas tree?

Liam: Yeah.

Sampson: Well, I didn't.

What do you get if you cross a Christmas tree with an apple?

A pineapple

What does Frosty the Snowman hang on his Christmas tree?

Icicles

How do Christmas trees get in to their computers?

They log in.

Which U.S. president liked Christmas decorations the most?

Tree-adore Roosevelt

What did the Christmas tree say to the ornament?

"Do you ever get tired of hanging around?"

Why is an elephant like a car and a Christmas tree?

They all have trunks.

What do you call a scared Christmas tree?

Petrified wood

What did the beaver say to the Christmas tree?

"Nice gnawing you!"

What is a Christmas tree's favorite Broadway musical?

My Fir Lady

Why are Christmas trees more noticeable on Christmas?

They have more presence.

What did the tree skirt say to the Christmas tree?

"I've got you covered!"

Knock, knock.

Who's there?

Tree.

Tree who?

Tree more days until Christmas vacation.

How did the Christmas tree get lost?

It took the wrong root.

What do you get when you cross a pig with a Christmas tree?

A pork-u-pine

Why do Christmas trees recycle?

They are evergreen.

How does a Christmas tree keep its breath fresh?

With orna-mints

Which former U.S. president planted the most Christmas trees?

Wood-row Wilson

How did the boy cut down the Christmas tree without going near it?

He saw it with his own two eyes.

Knock, knock.

Who's there?

Arnie.

Arnie who?

Arnie-ments are fun to put on the tree.

What did the umpire say when he was cutting down a Christmas tree?

"Tree strikes and you're out!"

What was Santa's best subject in high school?

Chemis-tree

Why did the Christmas tree go to the barber?

It needed to be trimmed.

What gets a new ring every year?

A Christmas tree

What did the porcupine say to the Christmas tree?

"Is that you, Mom?"

Did you hear about the Christmas tree who could play guitar?

Its name was Spruce Springsteen.

Which Canadian city is a favorite vacation spot for Christmas trees?

Mon-tree-al

What type of Christmas tree is green, has needles, and has a trunk that latches?

A Christmas tree going on vacation

Why did the Christmas tree go to the dentist?

He needed a root canal.

What is another name for an artificial Christmas tree?

Faux fir

RIB-TICKLING REINDEER

What is a female reindeer's favorite ice-cream flavor?

Cookie doe

Why didn't Rudolph get a good report card?

Because he went down in history

What do reindeer say before they tell you a joke?

"This one's gonna sleigh you!"

Who is an astronomer's favorite reindeer?

Comet

Knock, knock.

Who's there?

Olive.

Olive who?

"Olive the other reindeer . . ."

Why does Rudolph have a red nose?

Because he sneezes a lot

What does Rudolph do when Santa drives too fast?

He holds on for deer life!

Phil: Santa decided to give his reindeer a year off, so he got eight monkeys to pull his sleigh—Do, Re, Fa, So, La, Ti, and Do.

Will: What about Mi?

Phil: Oh, are you a monkey, too?

Where do Santa's reindeer stop for coffee?

Star-bucks

Which reindeer loves Valentine's Day?

Cupid

What do reindeer have that no other animals have?

Baby reindeer

Why do reindeer wear fur coats?

Because they look silly in snowsuits

What's the difference between a reindeer and a knight?

One slays the dragon, the other drags the sleigh.

Why is Blitzen always wet?

Because he's a rain-deer

Elf: Santa, I want to know how long reindeer should be groomed.

Santa: The same way as short ones.

What do you call a really smart reindeer?

A brain-deer

If a reindeer lost its tail, where would it go for a new one?

A retail shop

Why do Santa's reindeer fly?

Because they can't drive

Which reindeer loves to tango?

Dancer

Ted: I can lift a reindeer with one hand.

Tod: I'll bet you can't.

Ted: Find me a one-handed reindeer, and I'll show you!

Did you hear about the group of reindeer who got into trouble?

Yes, I herd!

How does Rudolph know when Christmas is coming?

He refers to his calen-deer.

Why did the reindeer stand on the marshmallow?

Because he didn't want to fall into the hot chocolate

What does it cost to get Santa's sleigh around the world?

Eight or nine bucks

Olivia: What do you call a reindeer with no eyes?

Tory: I have no eye-deer.

Olivia: What do you call a reindeer with no eyes and no legs?

Tory: Still no eye-deer.

How do you get into Donner's house?

You ring the deer-bell.

Why was Rudolph directing the Christmas play?

Because Santa asked him: "Won't you guide my play tonight?"

Which reindeer have the shortest legs?

The smallest ones

Why don't you see many reindeer in zoos?

Because they can't afford a ticket

Who helps deliver Christmas gifts to New England?

Maine-deer

Merry: Did Rudolph the Red-Nosed Reindeer have another nickname?

Holly: Yes. *Names.*

Merry: Where did you hear that?

Holly: In the song. "All of the other reindeer used to laugh and call him Names."

How do you get down from a reindeer?

You can't. You can only get down from a goose.

Which reindeer puts his elbows on the table?

Rude-olph

Who did the reindeer invite to his Christmas party?

His nearest and deer-est friends

What do you call a reindeer with three eyes?

A reiiindeer

Why does Scrooge love all of the reindeer?

Because every buck is dear to him!

NORTH POLE PUNS

**What would you do if you were trapped
on an iceberg at the North Pole?**

Just chill.

Why was the turkey asked to join the North Pole band?

Because it had the drumsticks

What nationality is Santa?

North Polish

What do you call a bird that stays at the North Pole all winter?

A brrrrrd

Why does St. Nicholas have a white beard?

So he can hide at the North Pole!

What does Santa use when he goes fishing?

His north pole

Who works construction at the North Pole?

The crane-deer

Where do polar bears vote?

The North Poll

What falls at the North Pole but doesn't get hurt?

Snow

How does Santa take pictures of his elves?

Using a North Pole-aroid camera

How do you know when Santa's at the North Pole?

You can always sense his presents.

What do North Pole road crews use?

Snow cones

What kind of burgers are served at the North Pole?

Ice-burgers

What is red and green and guides Santa's sleigh?

Rudolph the red-nosed pickle

What do you call a lion at the North Pole?

Lost

Where do Santa and the elves go swimming?

In the north pool

What did the Christmas tree wear for the North-Pole plunge?

Swimming trunks

SANTA
HA-HAS

What goes Oh, Oh, Oh?

Santa skiing backwards.

Knock, knock.

Who's there?

Huff.

Huff who?

**Huff you heard the news?
Santa Claus is coming to town!**

What do you call Santa when he stops moving?

Santa Pause

**What did the ghost say
to Santa?**

*"We'll have a boo
Christmas without you."*

How does Santa keep his hands clean?

He uses hand santa-tizer.

**What's red and white and
goes up and down and up
and down?**

Santa Claus in an elevator

Why did Santa put a clock in his sleigh?

Because he wanted to see time fly!

How do you know Santa Claus is good at karate?

He has a black belt.

What do you call Saint Nick after he slides down the chimney?

Cinder Claus

What is Santa's favorite state?

Idaho-ho-ho

What do you get when Santa plays detective?

Santa clues

What's as big as Santa but weighs nothing?

His shadow

What did Mrs. Claus say to Santa Claus?

"It looks like rain, dear."

Knock, knock.

Who's there?

Hair combs.

Hair combs who?

"Hair combs Santa Claus, right down Santa Claus lane!"

What's black, white, and red all over?

Santa Claus after he comes down the chimney

What's Santa's favorite snack food?

Crisp Pringles

Why did Santa go to the doctor?

Because of his bad 'elf!

What's the difference between Santa and a sled dog?

Santa wears a two-piece suit and a dog just pants.

What do you call a bankrupt Santa?

Saint Nickel-less

Where does Santa go to learn to slide down chimneys?

The chim-nasium

Knock, knock.

Who's there?

Ditty.

Ditty who?

Ditty see Santa Claus or not?

What do you call Santa's little helpers?

Subordinate clauses

Where do Santa's hats get made?

Man-hat-tan

Why did Santa wear sunglasses to the Christmas party?

Because he didn't want to be recognized

Who delivers Christmas presents to elephants?

Elephanta Claus

Why is Santa like a great coach?

He's always behind his team!

What does Santa like to have for breakfast?

Mistle-toast

Where does Santa keep his suit?

In his Claus-et

Knock, knock.

Who's there?

Annie.

Annie who?

Annie cookies and milk left for Santa?

What's red and white and falls down the chimney?

Santa Klutz

How much did Santa pay for his sleigh?

Nothing. It was on the house.

What do you say to Santa when he's taking attendance at school?

"Present."

Why does Santa Claus like to work in the garden?

Because he likes to hoe, hoe, hoe

How does Santa smell?

With his nose

Why did Mrs. Claus have to iron Santa's suit?

Because it was all Kringled

What does Santa suffer from whenever he gets stuck in a chimney?

Santa Claus-trophobia

How did Santa know he would marry Mrs. Claus?

It was love at frost sight!

Knock, knock.

Who's there?

Rhino.

Rhino who?

Rhino Santa lives at the North Pole. Do you know where he is?

What did the jet pilot say when Santa flew right in front of him, shouting "Merry Christmas"?

"Whew! That was a Claus call!"

What is Santa's favorite painting?

The Starry Night

Why does Santa go down the chimney on Christmas Eve?

Because it soots him

What do you get when you cross Santa Claus with a space ship?

A UF-ho-ho-ho!

What's Santa's dog's name?

Santa Paws

What's red and white and gives presents to gazelles?

Santelope

What happens when St. Nick's GPS doesn't work?

It's a lost Claus!

What's black, white, and red all over?

A zebra dressed up like Santa Claus

What kind of motorcycle does Santa ride?

A Holly Davidson

What do you call a clock with Santa's face on it?

The St. Nick of time

Where does Santa stay when he goes on vacation?

At a ho-ho-ho-tel

Why does St. Nick have so many wrinkles around his eyes?

Because when he laughs, Kris crinkles

Knock, knock.

Who's there?

Murray.

Murray who?

Murray Christmas to all, and to all a good night!

Sam: Is there a hole in your Christmas stocking?

Ty: No.

Sam: Then how will Santa put anything inside?

GIFTY GIGGLES

How is a mummy like a Christmas gift?

Both are wrapped.

Adelaide: I made these socks for my brother at college.

Mikayla: They're lovely, but why did you knit three socks?

Adelaide: In his last letter, he said he'd grown another foot!

Why did Santa cross the road?

To deliver presents!

What's the absolute best Christmas present?

A broken drum—you can't beat it!

Knock, knock.

Who's there?

Water.

Water who?

Water you want for Christmas?

How does a lump of coal start a story?

"Once upon a mine . . ."

Joe: What are you going to give your sister for Christmas?

Jack: I don't know. She wants something with diamonds on it.

Joe: How about a deck of cards?

What is a robot's favorite stocking stuffer?

Mixed nuts

What is a toy top's favorite food?

Spin-ach

Knock, knock.

Who's there?

Tamara.

Tamara who?

Tamara we will have to clean up all this wrapping paper.

Why didn't the rope get any Christmas presents?

It was knotty.

What did the lobster give to his teacher for Christmas?

A crab apple

Kylee: Merry Christmas, Grandma!

Grandma: Why did you give me a bunch of scrap paper?

Kylee: Because I love you to pieces!

Where do you find a Christmas present for a cat?

In a catalog

Knock, knock.

Who's there?

Frankfurter.

Frankfurter who?

Frankfurter lovely Christmas present.

What kind of Christmas stocking does a pirate have?

Arrrgyle

What do you call a dog who gets a lot of Christmas presents?

A golden receiver

Why does Santa take presents to children around the world?

Because the presents won't take themselves!

What did the rabbit give to his wife for Christmas?

A 14-carrot necklace

Knock, knock.

Who's there?

Doughnut.

Doughnut who?

Doughnut open this until Christmas.

What do you say when you give someone a set of spices for Christmas?

"Seasonings greetings!"

Who delivers presents to baby sharks at Christmas?

Santa Jaws

What gift do students give their teachers for Christmas?

Hot chalk-olate

Chicken #1: I hope our aunt gets her Christmas card in time.

Chicken #2: Don't worry. I sent it by eggs-press mail.

What kind of elephant can you find in a Christmas stocking?

A very small one

Knock, knock.

Who's there?

Lena.

Lena who?

Lena little closer and I'll tell you what I got you for Christmas.

When do you use a bow without an arrow?

When you're wrapping a present

What did the mouse give the other mouse for Christmas?

A Christ-mouse card

What kind of toy likes to rap?

A yo-yo

Jamie: What's the difference between a paper shredder and a mailbox?

Tim: I don't know.

Jamie: Well, I'll never send you out to mail the Christmas cards!

What do you get if you give a dinosaur a pogo stick for Christmas?

Big holes in your driveway

What did the stamp say to the Christmas card?

"Stick with me, and we'll go places!"

Knock, knock.

Who's there?

Canoe.

Canoe who?

Canoe hand me a piece of tape to wrap this present?

How many presents can Santa fit in an empty sack?

One—after he puts one in, it isn't empty anymore.

What did one telephone give to the other telephone for Christmas?

A ring

What kind of bow can't you put on a Christmas present?

An elbow

Luke: You know that alarm clock you gave me for Christmas?

Janie: Yes, Luke.

Luke: I had to take it back. It kept waking me up while I was sleeping.

What did the bald man say when he got a comb for Christmas?

"Thanks, I'll never part with it."

Knock, knock.

Who's there?

Rabbit.

Rabbit who?

Please rabbit up for me—it's a present for my mom.

Which dinosaur wrapped Christmas presents the fastest?

Veloci-wrapper

Carlos: What are you going to give your little brother for Christmas this year?

Maria: I'm not sure yet.

Carlos: What did you give him last year?

Maria: The chicken pox.

Knock, knock.

Who's there?

Quarter.

Quarter who?

Quarter trying to open her presents before Christmas!

What do frogs like to get in the mail at Christmas?

Flyers

What happened when the farmer gave the cow a Christmas present?

She was udderly delighted!

After the first two Wise Men presented their gifts of gold and frankincense, what did the third one say?

"Wait! There's myrrh!"

Knock, knock.

Who's there?

Yule.

Yule who?

Yule be sorry if you open your presents before Christmas!

Why is it getting harder to buy Advent calendars?

Because their days are numbered

NEW YEAR'S CHEER

What does the toad say on New Year's Eve?

"Hoppy New Year!"

What do vampires sing on New Year's Eve?

"Auld Fang Syne"

What did the mother pill say to the baby pill when the guests arrived on New Year's Eve?

"Aren't you going to vitamin?"

What do farmers give their wives at midnight on New Year's Eve?

Hogs and kisses

Knock, knock.

Who's there?

Mary and Abby.

Mary and Abby who?

Mary Christmas and Abby New Year!

Why do you need a jeweler on New Year's Eve?

To ring in the new year

What does one clock say to another clock on New Year's Day?

"You're getting older by the minute."

How can you find your way to the New Year's party?

Follow the "Auld Lang Sign."

What's the best New Year's resolution?

1080p

Why should you put your new calendar in the freezer?

To start off the new year in a cool way

What did the cheerleaders say on New Year's Day?

"Happy New Cheer!"

Where is New Year's Eve very mathematical?

Times Square

What do you say to someone when you see them after the ball drops on New Year's?

"I haven't seen you since last year!"

Knock, knock.

Who's there?

Moo.

Moo who?

Happy Moo Year!

What should you never eat on New Year's Eve?

Fire crackers

Why did the boy put a slice of bread in the oven at midnight on December 31?

He wanted to make a New Year's toast.

What did the cat say at midnight on New Year's?

"Meow."

What is corn's favorite holiday?

New Ear's Day!

Why does the person who runs Times Square on New Year's feel like a failure?

He always drops the ball.

What does a ghost say on January 1?

"Happy BOO year!"

Why did the grocer put a Christmas sale on vegetables?

He wanted to give peas a chance!

What time is it when the clock strikes 13 on New Year's Eve?

Time to fix the clock

What did Adam say to his wife on January 1?

"It's New Year's, Eve!"

What comes at the end of New Year's Day?

The letter "Y"

LAST LAUGHS

What is a mushroom's favorite Christmas vacation spot?

Port-a-bella

Where does an angel get his milk?

From holy cows

Knock, knock.

Who's there?

Lois.

Lois who?

Lois shelf is where I keep the Christmas cookies.

How does a monster greet her friends during the holidays?

"Scary Christmas!"

Sandra: My son came to visit for Christmas.

Sally: How nice. Did you meet him at the airport?

Sandra: Goodness, no. I've known him for years!

Knock, knock.

Who's there?

Aviary.

Aviary who?

Aviary Merry Christmas to you!

What does everyone start Christmas Day with?

The letter "C"

Where did the pilgrims celebrate Christmas?

Jingle Bell Rock

Knock, knock.

Who's there?

Icy.

Icy who?

Icy a big polar bear.

What's the difference between the Christmas alphabet and the ordinary alphabet?

The Christmas alphabet has No-el.

Knock, knock.

Who's there?

Christmas.

Christmas who?

Christmas shovel the driveway today.

How does Sir Galahad's favorite poem start?

'Twas the Knight before Christmas . . .

Knock, knock.

Who's there?

Woodchuck.

Woodchuck who?

Woodchuck come to Christmas dinner if we invited him?

Why did Scrooge take his clock to the bank?

He was trying to save time.

Who do you call if your sink breaks on Christmas?

The little plumber boy

What is a polar bear's favorite ride at the amusement park?

The polar coaster

Knock, knock.

Who's there?

Isolate.

Isolate who?

Isolate to the Christmas party—I almost missed it!

Why couldn't the skeleton go to the Christmas party?

He had nobody to go with.

How does a soccer ball greet its friends on Christmas?

"Season's Cleat-ings!"

Where can you see the best Christmas videos?

On Yule-Tube

Knock, knock.

Who's there?

Peas.

Peas who?

Peas on Earth!

Where does Christmas come before Thanksgiving?

In the dictionary

Emma: How does waiting for Christmas keep you in suspense?

Noah: I don't know. How?

Emma: I'll tell you tomorrow.

Knock, knock.

Who's there?

Igloo.

Igloo who?

Igloo came over for Christmas, you'd have a good time.

How did Scrooge win the soccer match?

The ghost of Christmas passed.

How did Sofia greet her father on Christmas morning?

"Feliz Navi-Dad!"

Why did the golfer buy two Christmas stockings?

In case he got a hole in one

Jordan: It was a stormy Christmas Eve. I was walking down the road when two piecosts started to cross the street.

Aliya: What's a piecost?

Jordan: About five dollars.

Knock, knock.

Who's there?

Christmas.

Christmas who?

Christmas be my lucky day to see all my family members!

Where does the Ghost of Christmas Present spend Christmas?

The Boo-hamas

Corn Cob #1: You're invited to my Christmas party!

Corn Cob #2: Aw, shucks. Thanks!

How do angels greet each other?

"Halo!"

Knock, knock.

Who's there?

Pizza.

Pizza, who?

Pizza on earth, good will toward all!

Knock, knock.

Who's there?

Noah.

Noah who?

Noah good joke about Christmas?

Why did the elf say "knock, knock"?

He was in the wrong joke.

Did you hear the joke about the Christmas tree?

Never mind, it was sappy.

What did the peanut butter say to the grape on Christmas?

"'Tis the season to be jelly!"

What do you call a snowman who does sit-ups?

An abdominal snowman

What do sheep say to shepherds at Christmastime?

"Season's bleatings!"

Why did the snowman wear a suit of armor to the comedy show?

To protect himself from the punch lines

Knock, knock.

Who's there?

Thistle.

Thistle who?

Thistle be the last joke in the book!